The Wrapping Scarf Revolution

The Earth-Friendly Idea that Will Change
the Way You Think About Your World

by Patricia Lee

LEISURE ARTS, INC.
Little Rock, Arkansas

Vice President and Chief Operations Officer: Tom Siebenmorgen
Vice President, Sales and Marketing: Pam Stebbins
Vice President, Operations: Jim Dittrich
Editor-in-Chief: Susan White Sullivan
Director of Designer Relations: Debra Nettles
Senior Art Director: Rhonda Shelby
Senior Prepress Director: Mark Hawkins

Lee, Patricia
The Wrapping Scarf Revolution: The Earth-Friendly Idea that Will Change the Way You Think About Your World/ by Patricia Lee- 1st ed.

Library of Congress Control Number: 2009928440
ISBN 13: 978-1-57486-106-8
ISBN 10: 1-57486-106-9

Bojagi *on previous page by artist Bokhee Kim*

For my parents, Kay and H.T.

Contents

A Gift Wrapped in Wisdom

Christmas morning. The most magical day of the year. On this particular morning, I found myself sighing with disgust as I glared at a huge pile of torn and crumpled wrapping paper, the carnage leftover from an otherwise perfect family celebration. As I gathered up the garbage and dragged it outside to my already overflowing trash can, I thought about how many other homes must be putting similar mountains of barely used paper into their trash at that very moment. I remembered the beautiful reusable wrapping scarves I saw people use in Korea to wrap gifts and wondered why in the world something like that wasn't available here.

A little research through the Clean Air Council revealed that in the United States alone, an additional five million tons of waste is generated during the winter holidays; four million tons of this is wrapping paper and shopping bags. Shocked at these staggering numbers, I decided that the time had come for me to do what little I could to "stop the carnage" in my home.

Love at First Sight

My love affair with the wrapping scarf started when I visited Korea as a freshman in college. During my two month stay in Seoul, I was lucky enough to live with my aunt who taught me so much about the Korean way of life. One day, as Auntie Min prepared to go to a friend's house, she brought out a big box of luxurious ginseng teas to give to the hostess as a gift. However, instead of gathering the usual supplies of wrapping paper, tape, scissors, and gift bag, I stared in amazement as she casually took a pretty pink scarf from a pile of similar scarves in a drawer and proceeded to wrap the box of teas with the scarf using two simple knots that held everything together. She then picked up the wrapped package by the knots as if she were picking up a bag by the handles and headed for the door. I was nothing short of astonished. Not only was it so simple, it was so beautiful!

Having grown up in a traditional Korean household of four generations, I was no stranger to wrapping scarves, or *bojagi* (BOH-jog-ee) as they are called in Korea. In the spring, my grandmother and great-grandmother wrapped up all our sweaters and comforters and put them away for the season. When bringing food to a sick neighbor, they put the dishes in containers and wrapped up the whole stack with a single *bojagi*. But before that summer in Korea, I had never seen the wrapping scarf used so elegantly.

When I commented on what a genius she was, Auntie Min gave me a look of bewilderment and seemed to think that I was making fun of her. Little did I know then that the *bojagi* was the traditional way of wrapping things in Korea, and that most modern folks considered this practice to be quite old fashioned and even a bit frumpy. Auntie Min was a wonderful paradox of

Bojagi on this page and facing page by Bokhee Kim

extravagant tastes and frugal habits. She was always on the trail of the latest designer labels and willing to shell out the dough, yet had a fear of wastefulness that bordered on paranoia. Leftovers never thoughtlessly went in the trash and the use of paper towels instead of rags was a silly extravangance in her mind. In many ways, she embodied the modern Korean woman who enjoyed her hard-earned prosperity but never forgot the dire poverty that gripped the whole nation in her youth.

One of the most fascinating lessons that I learned in Korea was how quickly the nation was able to recover from abject poverty following the double tragedies of Japanese colonization and the Korean War. The vivid imagery of millions of refugees fleeing the Communists with their possessions wrapped in *bojagi* is one that is still painful for many older Koreans. In 1953 when Auntie Min was ten years old, the per capita income in Korea was just $87. Unfathomable to many of us who often carry that much cash in our wallets, how is it that Korea was able to recover so quickly to become the world's 13th largest economy and one of the top wired nations in the world?

Over and over again, during my summer stay in Seoul, I would be struck by the Korean people's strong aversion to waste. Men, women, and even children still used the wrapping scarf in one form or another. Children wrapped their lunch in *bojagi*, attorneys carried stacks of paper in it, and merchants used it to protect and transport all kinds of goods. To them, the multifunctioning wrapping scarf was an indispensible tool in their daily lives. Though the wrapping scarf was sometimes a reminder of a painful past full of suffering and hard times, the deeply rooted tenets of industriousness and resourcefulness could not be suppressed, and helped propel a nation devastated by war and poverty to prosperity in one generation.

What did we do before we used disposable products?

Back at Home

When I got back to the states as a full-time art student, I couldn't wait to start wrapping up all my gifts with this great new idea. My thought was that I could just take scarves available in stores and use the knotting techniques that I learned in Korea. While it was fun to experiment and share the idea with friends, I couldn't quite achieve the look that I had in my mind. The magic that I witnessed in the beautiful yet practical wrapping scarves of Korea wasn't so easily attained after all. I fantasized about buying fabrics and making my own but, as an Apparel Design 101 drop-out, I lacked the skills and time to realize my vision.

Fast forward twenty years to that fateful Christmas morning and I finally decided that it was high time I took some action in making my wrapping scarf dreams a reality. With the intention of giving wrapping scarves to all my friends and family, I went to the garment district in New York City and had a prototype made of exactly the kind of wrapping scarf that I wanted to use. I called them "bobos" as a play on the word *bojagi*. I was having so much fun choosing fabrics and making samples that before I knew it, I had a solid collection of products that my friends and family could not get enough of. The BOBO Wrapping Scarf Company was born and I was on a mission.

I just knew that the time was right for America to embrace this idea that not only reduced waste but transformed the traditional approach to wrapping and carrying things in general. While the Western view of gift wrapping involves cutting and taping disposable paper to fit an item, then finding the right disposable bag to carry and transport the item, the wrapping scarf actually transforms itself to adapt to whatever it is wrapping, and at the same time becomes its own bag complete with handles. What's more, it can then be used for these purposes and more, over and over again. The multi-functionality and reusability of the wrapping scarf makes so much sense in this era of environmental crisis.

Consumption Gone Wild

It is clear that most of us have been speeding down the road of consumption in a world that seems to equate quality of life with how much we consume. This kind of thinking is based on a critical disconnect between us, the consumer, and the natural world. We have become so separated from our roots that we rarely incorporate the wisdom of our ancestors in building the substance of our lives. In looking for ways to live more sustainably, one question that the wrapping scarf answers so well is: What did we do before we used disposable products?

Fritjof Capra, renowned physicist and author of the *Tao of Physics*, tells us that we need a paradigm shift from our Western Cartesian world view in which we were thought to all be separate entities, to a new vision of reality that inextricably connects the individual to the cosmos as a whole. He looks to the ancient wisdom of the East as the most consistent philosophical background to this most modern of scientific theories which at its core supports ecological sustainability. The Korean *bojagi* is the perfect example of this kind of thinking where we relate to our world with flexibility and openness. *Bojagi* can be used to wrap and carry clothes to the laundry or to provide shade in a sunny window. It carries your food to a picnic, then becomes the blanket that you sit on. Always ready to adapt to your needs, it is the perfect accessory for simple human living. Ironically, our era is one in which the East continues to be more and more influenced by Western attitudes toward rigid specialization and high speed consumption.

While it's easy to feel overwhelmed with how much we aren't doing right, we can all take baby steps in the right direction. It is my hope that through this book I can inspire you in the way my Auntie Min inspired me, and spur you on to share this one great idea with everyone you know. Eventually I hope that our enthusiasm here in the West will rekindle interest in the East where the wrapping scarf is, sadly, a fading tradition.

Japan, which has its own great tradition of wrapping scarves, has in motion a national agenda to promote the revival of wrapping scarves in an effort to stem the use of disposable products. Korea charges a severe tax on the purchase of each garbage bag that households are allowed to use while providing recycling services free nationwide. In Ireland, a tax on plastic shopping bags cut their use by more than 90%, and Bangladesh banned the use of polyethylene bags because they were blocking drainage systems – a major culprit in at least two disastrous floods. China's recent ban on plastic bags will save 37 million barrels of oil every year.

The wrapping scarf revolution is all about reducing the waste in our lives while still celebrating beauty and fine things. It's about learning to do things with our hands and saying no to the impatience and mindlessness that encourage a disposable culture. It is also a way to connect with not only the cultures of the East, but to all the cultures of the world who are finding new and old ways to heal our damaged planet.

The Basics

A Brief History of the Wrapping Scarf

The oldest surviving *bojagi* dates back to the 11th century and was the property of an illustrious Buddhist monk. Recorded history tells us that the Korean wrapping scarf or *bojagi* was used extensively during the Joseon Dynasty (1392-1910) as a way for women to utilize small scraps of fabric left over from the making of clothing and other goods. The little pieces were sewn together by hand to create a beautiful quilt-like scarf that was used in many ways around the home. Ingeniously adaptable and easy to store, *bojagi* was used to wrap, store, cover, and transport all the things that were essential to everyday life. Rich, poor, young and old, everyone used *bojagi*. Although there were countless ways to use *bojagi*, the formal and artistic wrapping of items became a very important, even sacred, part of the culture.

Koreans believed that the careful wrapping of things not only showed respect and honor but also brought luck and good fortune to the recipient of a wrapped gift, especially in the case of a wedding. During the Joseon period, couples were married at a very young age with boys often quite a bit younger than the girls. Boys were commonly married at the age of 12 and girls at the age of 16. The marriage was arranged by the families of the

Antique wrapping scarf from the 19th century, artist unknown, size 35 x 35 inches

bride and groom and elaborate gift-giving between the in-laws was and still remains an important part of the Korean marriage tradition.

The word *bo* means to cover and protect, and the *bojagi's* main function is to do just that. The official gift from the groom's family to the bride's family is delivered in a gift chest called a *hahm* which is specially wrapped and delivered in a *hahm-bo*. Always included in the *hahm* is blue and red

silk which symbolizes the woman and the man respectively. The blue silk is wrapped in red and tied with blue string. The red silk is wrapped in blue and tied with red string. This represents the harmonious union between the man and the woman while the string signifies the binding of the two into one.

Ancient Koreans were so enamored with the lifelong devotion and monogamy of wild geese that a ceremonial pair of wooden geese became an important part of all Korean weddings. The wooden geese are wrapped in a red and blue *bojagi* called *kirogi-bo* and are presented by the groom to the bride's family at the beginning of the wedding as a symbol of his faithfulness.

Apart from formal occasions, the *bojagi* not only wrapped gifts but was used as bag, box, suitcase, and multipurpose covering. Tables, or *sahng,* were covered with *sahng-bo* and blankets not in use were covered with a blanket wrap or *ibul-bo*. It was considered rude and disrespectful to pay anyone or hand anyone a gift of money directly without a special covering called the money-wrap, or *dohn-bo*. This tradition still lives on today though the disposable envelope has largely replaced the *dohn-bo*.

The wrapping scarf tradition really blossomed and became an art form in Korea, but as long as human beings had belongings to carry, it seems likely that ancient people of all cultures used some form of wrapping scarf to wrap and carry their goods from place to place. Women in Africa often carry bundles of things wrapped in colorful cloth, and even in the iconography of America's early days, the carefree wanderer is often seen carrying his little bundle of wrapped-up belongings on a stick. Japanese wrapping scarves have a rich history all their own and were originally used as a means to carry personal items to the public bath house.

Hanbok illustrations on this page, facing page, and page 24, Kim Yong-suk and Son Kyong-ja, "An Illustrated History of Korean Costume, Volume II", Ye-kyong, 1984, p. 43, 87, 95

Unique to Korean wrapping scarves, many *bojagi* have long strips of cloth attached to the corners to facilitate the wrapping of larger items. These strips were also used to tie the *bojagi* onto table legs when covering food that had been set on traditional portable dining tables.

Surviving antique *bojagi* from the Joseon dynasty show that traditional Korean wrapping scarves came in many different shapes, sizes, and styles. While many feature the artistic arranging of fabric pieces to create beautiful designs, others used in more formal settings are single or double sheets of silk or ramie printed with natural dyes and gold leaf. Embroidery was an integral part of a cultured woman's education and many of the intricately embroiderd *bojagi* that survive to this day show no signs of use. This indicates that decorative *bojagi* were often made as works to be admired and perhaps passed down through the generations as treasured heirlooms. The quilt-like wraps made of many small pieces are called *jogak-bo*, and the embroidered wraps are called *su-bo*.

Single layer *bojagi* in Korea are called *hoht-bo* and are used for everyday wrapping, protecting and carrying. Many of the decorative wrapping scarves used in Korea are lined with inner and outer sheets of contrasting colors. These are called *kyop-bo* and reflect the layered look of the traditional Korean dress, the *hanbok*.

Waste is considered to bring bad luck in Korea and the exquisite antique wrapping scarves made by the industrious hands of ancient Korean women are treasured as important cultural icons.

The Scarf

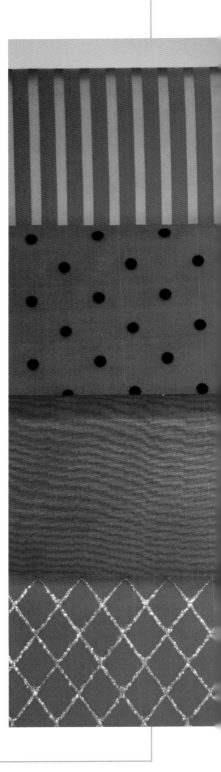

In a pinch, almost any squarish piece of material will work to tie up a package or make a quick bag. However, as is usually the case, the right tools produce the best results.

I love to use double-layered wrapping scarves for most of my gift wrapping, bag making, and decorative use. The contrasting color on the reverse provides an accent that really gives the wrapped item a beautifully finished look. To achieve this look with a single layered wrapping scarf, look for fabric that has a different color, pattern, or texture on the reverse.

Double layered chiffon or organza wrapping scarves are especially beautiful as the colors interact to produce rich and unexpected shades. Delicate and translucent, they feel like puffs of air and give gifts the look of a custom-made frock.

Simple single sheet wrapping scarves certainly have their place in various utilitarian uses and are more economical to buy and make. The single layered wrapping scarves are great for grocery shopping and general toting. Embellish with some accessories or ribbons for gift wrapping.

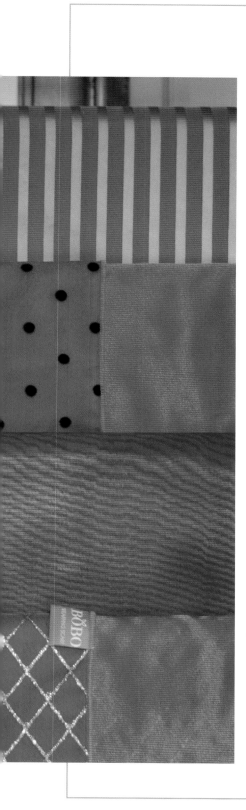

A useful wrap on the small end of the spectrum would be about 20-22 inches square, or roughly the size of a bandana. This would wrap a few CDs, a small box, a sachet, or make a cute tissue box cover.

A medium size for all-purpose wrapping would be about 27-30 inches square and a large wrapping scarf about 36 inches square would be great for wrapping two wine bottles. A 42-inch wrap makes a great slouchy hobo bag which can double as a grocery or shopping bag. Of course you can use larger sizes depending on the size of the item being wrapped. A very large wrapping scarf of 60 inches or so could wrap up a blanket or two that are going into storage or could be used to wrap, carry, or store large works of art.

The material used to make a wrapping scarf also varies depending on personal taste and intended use. Traditional Korean *bojagi* are made from silk, cotton, ramie, or hemp. For modern usage, synthetic fabrics and blends are the most practical in terms of use and care. Cotton can also be used successfully although significant wrinkling may be an issue. Silk material makes for a truly luxurious wrapping scarf that can be appropriate for making an evening bag or wrapping a very special gift. It makes sense to avoid materials that won't stand up to repeated washing. However, in the spirit of the original *bojagi*, it's great to be resourceful and use whatever you have on hand.

Bojagi at right by Bokhee Kim

How to Knot

If You Can Tie Your Shoes, You Can Tie a Wrapping Scarf

All the techniques covered in this book use three basic knots. The half knot, the single knot, and most importantly the square knot.

If you are already familiar with tying a square knot through boating, scouts, or fashion, you are way ahead of where I was when I first started. I was the kind of gal that loved origami but could never get those pesky folds just right even for the most basic shapes. After many attempts I realized that origami was not going to be my thing.

Folding and tying a wrapping scarf, on the other hand, looked just as beautiful and complex as origami, but turned out to be so much simpler. When I saw how quickly my kids learned to tie wrapping scarves, I realized that if you can tie your shoelaces, you can tie a wrapping scarf.

The half knot is two corners of a wrap tied together just once, as opposed to twice in a square knot.

The Half Knot and the Square Knot

1. Cross the green corner over the pink corner then loop it over and under the pink corner.

2. Here is your half knot.

Important!

3. Bend the pink corner over to the right before bringing the green corner over and under the pink corner to finish the square knot.

4. Pull corners to tighten and test to make sure the knot is secure.

Beware the Granny knot! It is very similar to the square knot but it is not secure. If you end up with a Granny knot, untie and try again.

The Single Knot

The ³/₄ Knot or the Hanbok Knot

This knot is a favorite knot of the Koreans and is used to tie the traditional Korean dress, the *hanbok*. The great thing about this knot is that it is so easy to untie and to me it represents a very Korean attitude of mixing beauty and practicality. This knot is more secure than a half knot but not as secure as a square knot.

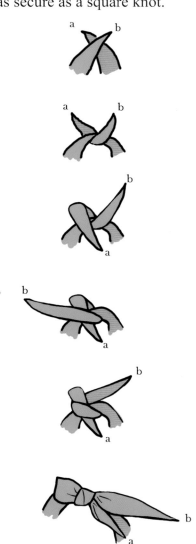

1. Cross corner b over corner a then loop it under and out of corner a.

2. Here is your half knot.

3. Bend corner as if you are going to tie a bow.

4. Pull corner b over corner a to the other side.

5. Wrap corner b around and behind corner a.

6. Pull corner b through the loop and pull tight.

The Twist

The seemingly simple maneuver of twisting the corners of a wrapping scarf to get a rope-like handle can be a little confusing at first.

The first step is to pull the corner taut to get a good line of material to twist. Lift up the wrapping scarf corner in a vertical position and twist the fabric from the base up, taking careful note of which way you are twisting. Then take the other corner, lift, and make sure to twist in the same direction, not opposite. Leave enough room at the ends to tie the corners in a square knot. When you've tied your corners together, play around with the finished handle(s) to make a rounded shape.

If the twist unravels easily, you probably twisted the two ends in opposite directions. It may take a little practice but it won't be long before you are a master of this technique which adds a beautiful texture and firmness to your handles.

Making the Perfect "Bow"

1. Cross corner b over corner a and make a half knot.

2. Cross corner a to the right making sure that the color you want showing is facing up. Loop corner b over and under corner a with the "wrong" side facing up. Make sure that corner b is longer than corner a so that the bows will be even in the end.

3. Pull corner b out of the knot with the correct side facing up. Straighten out your bow and make any final adjustments.

If you have a square knot that is very tight and are having trouble untying it, try pulling on one side of the bow to loosen the knot. Then ease the knot out.

Creative
Wrapping

Gift Wrapping

While some eco-minded folks encourage forgoing the gift wrap altogether, I think that the wrapping of gifts is a beautiful and important human tradition. There is an element of mystery and suspense which adds so much to the whole experience of showing one's affection and appreciation to another person. The trick is to not spoil the beauty with a whole lot of waste.

Whether the item being wrapped is a box, a cylinder, a bowl, or a combination of these things, there is a wrapping scarf technique suitable for the job. How hard is it to wrap a ball or any sphere with paper? With a wrapping scarf, it's almost magically simple and functional. Imagine a world where you pass along your favorite wrapping scarves to your favorite people and they pass it on until one day it may even come back to you!

While I love to give a wrapping scarf as part of a gift, I often just use it as a means of transporting a gift such as a cake in a pastry box and bring my wrapping scarf back home. You can also have your name monogrammed on a wrapping scarf so that your friends will return it to you much like a plate with a gift of food will be returned. In Asia, some people will unwrap the gift in front of the recipient and bring the wrapping scarf back home so that the recipient will not feel compelled to return the wrapping scarf with a reciprocal gift.

Any way you choose to use it, the wrapping scarf will become an integral part of your gift-giving.

The Lotus Wrap

To wrap a few CDs as shown below, use a small wrap that is about 20" x 20".

When learning how to use a wrapping scarf, this is the basic technique to master first. A simple two-step process of bringing together opposite corners of the scarf and tying square knots, this style creates a beautiful lotus-like bow at the top which also functions as a handle.

1. Place item in the center of the wrapping scarf on the diagonal.

2. Tie 2 opposite corners snugly in a square knot.

3. Bring up the remaining 2 corners and tie them in a square knot.

4. Arrange final knot to desired effect. Tuck away any loose fabric.

The Orchid Wrap
& Variations

My friend Julie and I were wrapping up gifts for a friend's piano recital when she mentioned that they looked like orchids. We've called this the orchid wrap ever since. Fluff out the petals at the end for maximum volume.

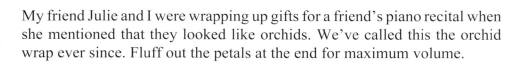

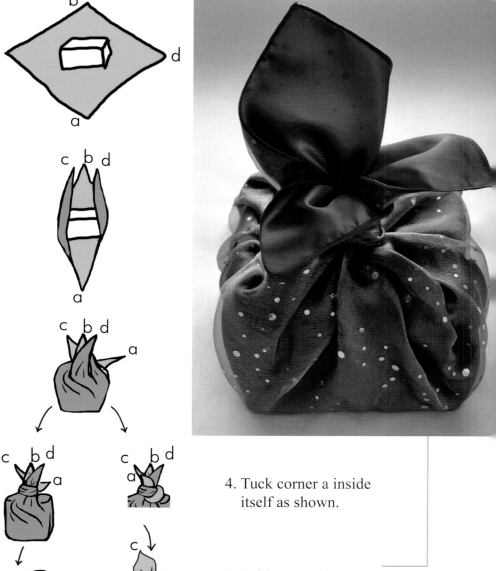

1. Place object in the center of the wrapping scarf on the diagonal.

2. Raise corners c, b, and d and hold with one hand.

3. Bring corner a behind corners c, b, and d, and wrap it around at the top of the box.

4. Tie corner a with corner c (or d or b) in a square knot.

5. Fold corners b and d down and arrange the petals.

4. Tuck corner a inside itself as shown.

5. Fold corners b, c, and d down and arrange the petals.

Here is a simpler version of the Orchid Wrap: On step 2, raise all 4 corners instead of 3 and tie with a decorative scrunchie or bungee tie.

To wrap a box of stationery as shown at left, use a small wrap that is about 20" x 20".

The Blooming Orchid Wrap

Take your gifts to another level of "wow!" This simple three-step technique gives whatever you're wrapping a beautiful sculptural effect.

1. Neatly bring up all four corners, two opposite corners at a time, and secure firmly with a bungee, ribbon, or rubber band.
2. Take two opposite corners and tuck into the center.
3. Fluff up the tucked sides to create volume.

The Bow Tie Wrap

Don't you love the crisp and dapper look of bow ties? I never did master the art of tying one, but here's one bow tie that anyone can manage.

1. Place object in the center of the wrapping scarf on the diagonal.

2. Raise corner d and drape over the object.

3. Repeat with corner b.

4. Neatly raise corners a and c and tie in a square knot. Leave as is to achieve look in Figure 2.

5. Optional: Raise corner b up and over the square knot and tuck under the knot (see Figure 1).

Figure 1

Figure 2

The Fancy Wrap
& Variation

Here are two ways to really dress up your gift. These techniques work best when the wrapping scarf is much bigger than the item being wrapped.

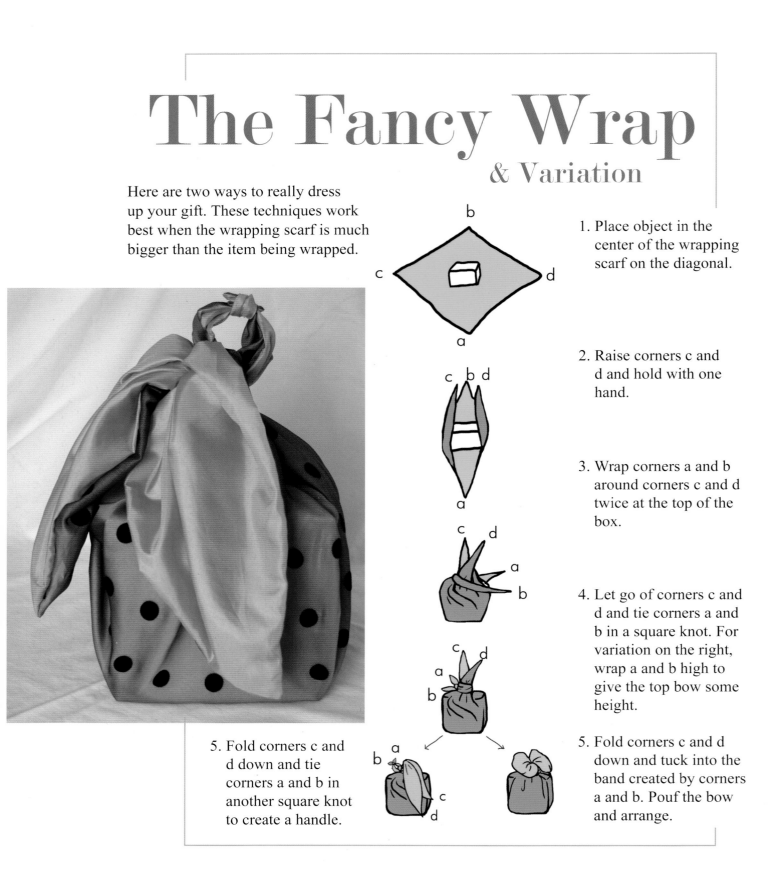

1. Place object in the center of the wrapping scarf on the diagonal.

2. Raise corners c and d and hold with one hand.

3. Wrap corners a and b around corners c and d twice at the top of the box.

4. Let go of corners c and d and tie corners a and b in a square knot. For variation on the right, wrap a and b high to give the top bow some height.

5. Fold corners c and d down and tie corners a and b in another square knot to create a handle.

5. Fold corners c and d down and tuck into the band created by corners a and b. Pouf the bow and arrange.

To wrap a 12" cube box, use a large wrap that is about 42" x 42".

To wrap this 24" x 4" cylinder, use a large wrap that is about 45" x 45".

The Cylinder Wrap

The Cylinder Wrap comes in very handy when you need to transport or store a rolled-up document, poster, or painting. The final steps depend on whether you'd like a tighter finish or a shoulder strap. The method at left also works well for a bottle of wine and both methods can be used to wrap long rectangular boxes.

The length of corner c to corner d should be three times the length of the cylinder. If scarf is too small, just tie corners c and d in a square knot in step 3.

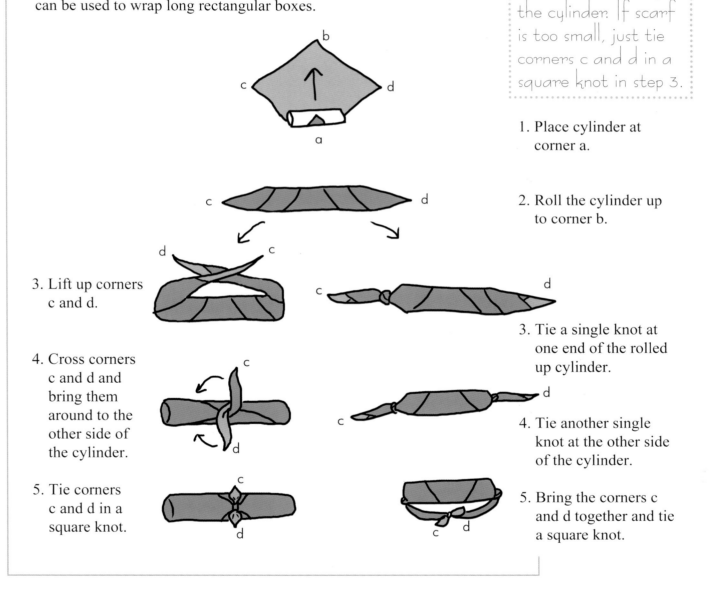

1. Place cylinder at corner a.

2. Roll the cylinder up to corner b.

3. Lift up corners c and d.

3. Tie a single knot at one end of the rolled up cylinder.

4. Cross corners c and d and bring them around to the other side of the cylinder.

4. Tie another single knot at the other side of the cylinder.

5. Tie corners c and d in a square knot.

5. Bring the corners c and d together and tie a square knot.

The Ball Wrap
& Variation

In Japan, this type of wrapping is called the watermelon wrap. When making the twisted handles in the second variation shown on the right, make sure to twist the two corners separately to form one rope before tying (see page 26). This will create a stiffer handle that is less prone to unraveling.

To wrap a basketball as shown, use a large wrap that is about 42" x 42".

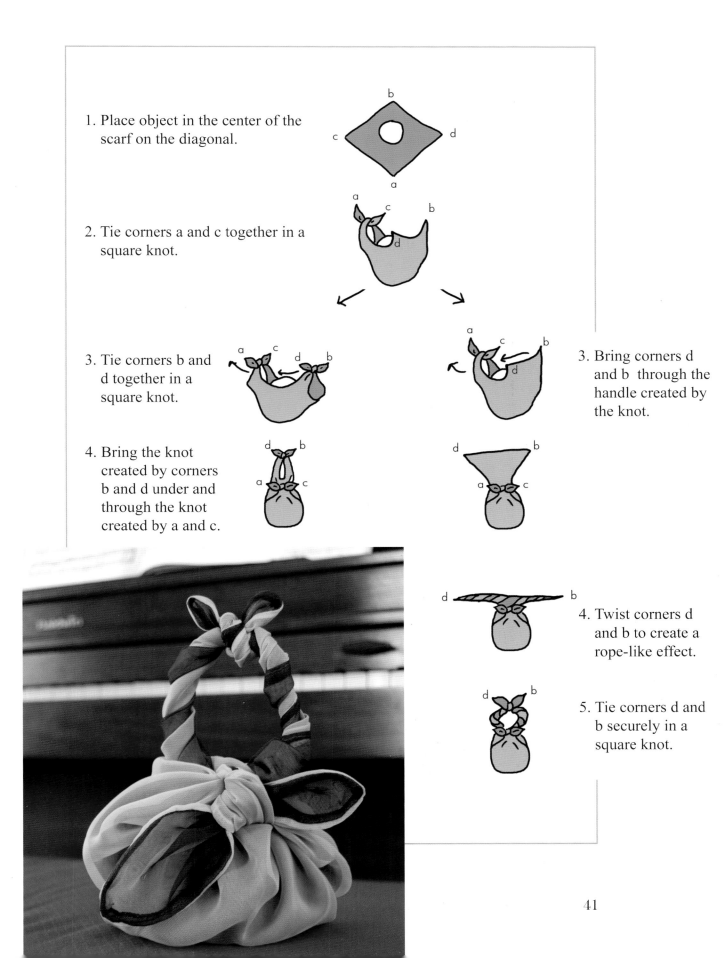

1. Place object in the center of the scarf on the diagonal.

2. Tie corners a and c together in a square knot.

3. Tie corners b and d together in a square knot.

4. Bring the knot created by corners b and d under and through the knot created by a and c.

3. Bring corners d and b through the handle created by the knot.

4. Twist corners d and b to create a rope-like effect.

5. Tie corners d and b securely in a square knot.

41

The Double Bow Wrap

I love the symmetry of The Double Bow Wrap, but it does require a bit of practice to get the bows to really mirror each other. This technique is also handy when the object being wrapped is on the large side compared to the wrapping scarf.

If you are short on time and your wrapping scarf is very wrinkled, try to at least iron the corners. That way all your bows will be nice and smooth.

1. Place item in the center of the wrapping scarf on the diagonal. Corners a and b should have more room than corners c and d.

2. Bring up corners a and b and cross them so that b is on the side of corner c. Corner a should be on the side of corner d.

3. Bring up corner c and tie with corner b in a square knot. Make sure that corner c goes over and under corner b.

4. Bring up corner d and tie with corner a in a square knot. Make sure that corner d goes over and under corner a.

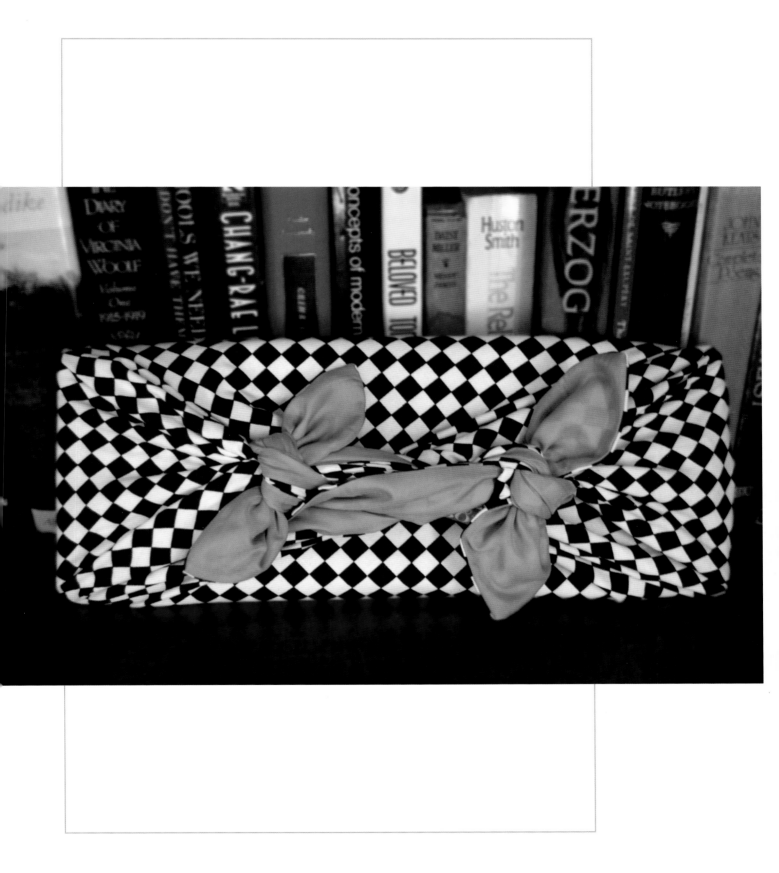

The Double Handle Wrap

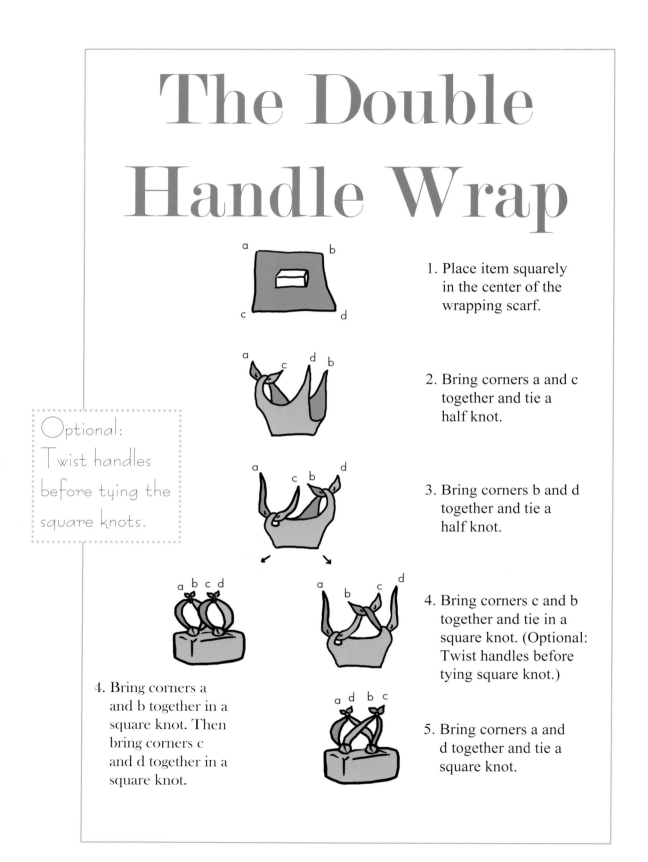

1. Place item squarely in the center of the wrapping scarf.

2. Bring corners a and c together and tie a half knot.

Optional: Twist handles before tying the square knots.

3. Bring corners b and d together and tie a half knot.

4. Bring corners c and b together and tie in a square knot. (Optional: Twist handles before tying square knot.)

4. Bring corners a and b together in a square knot. Then bring corners c and d together in a square knot.

5. Bring corners a and d together and tie a square knot.

The Double Handle Wrap is truly a beautifully wrapped gift and a bag in one. This is one time when you don't put the item being wrapped on the diagonal. The handles can be left plain or twisted for more texture. Make sure your square knots are tight so the handles don't come undone.

The Single Handle Wrap

This is another versatile wrap that works well when the wrapping scarf is much larger than the object being wrapped. I love the big floppy bow in the center and of course the handles can be left untwisted.

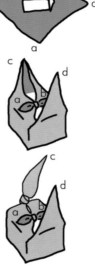

1. Place box (or other item) in the center of the wrapping scarf on the diagonal.

2. Tie corners a and b in a square knot.

3. Bring up corner c and tie a single knot at the top edge of the box.

4. Bring up corner d and tie a single knot at the top edge of the box.

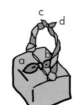

5. Pull corners c and d and twist. Tie together in a square knot.

Variation:

Follow steps 1 and 2. In step 3, do not tie single knots but bring up corners c and d and tie them in a half knot all the way down to the top of your box. Proceed to step 5. (Also shown on page 26.)

To wrap a wine bottle as shown, use a medium wrap that is about 28" x 28".

The One-Bottle Wrap & Carry

Elegant and practical, this is a great way to gift a bottle of wine or to carry around your water bottle. This also works well when wrapping any tall thin object like a trophy. I love the way a wrapping scarf adapts so beautifully to so many different shapes!

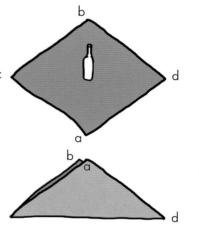

1. Stand the bottle in the center of the wrapping scarf on the diagonal.

2. Bring corners b and a together at top of the bottle.

3. Tie corners b and a in a half knot.

4. Bring corners b and a together again to make a handle. Tie a square knot.

5. Criss-cross corners c and d at the back of the bottle and bring around to the front.

6. Tie corners c and d in a square knot.

The Two-Bottle Wrap & Carry

My jaw nearly dropped to the floor when I saw this technique for wrapping up two bottles. Almost like a magic trick, this wrap works beautifully for all kinds of pairings such as oil and vinegar, candles, and jam. Whether you are giving your bottles as a gift, or you are taking them on a picnic, make sure your knot is secure and the material at the bottom is smooth and stable.

The wrapped-up bottles should feel quite secure when lifted. If the scarf is fitting too loosely, untie and try again.

1. Lay two bottles facing out in the middle of the wrapping scarf. Leave a little space in between the bottles.

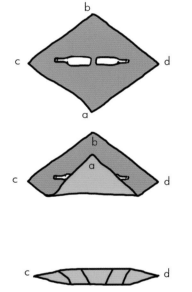

2. Bring up corner a to cover the bottles. Make sure the fabric is flush with the edge of the bottles.

3. Roll the bottles and the fabric up to corner b.

4. Stand the bottles up, bring up corners c and d.

5. Tie corners c and d in a secure square knot. Tuck away any loose fabric.

To wrap two wine bottles with a large floppy "bow" at the top as shown, use a large wrap that is about 42" x 42".

The smallest wrap you can use to wrap two wine bottles would be about 28" x 28".

Bags, Bags, Bags

Bags on Demand

From the most precious little evening wristlet to large heavy-duty grocery totes, you can make bags of many different sizes and shapes. Not sure how much grocery shopping you are going to be doing? Take a bunch of wrapping scarves, wrapped up in a wrapping scarf of course, and throw them in your purse. Another idea is to tie a pretty wrapping scarf on your purse and always have an extra "bag" handy.

The Simplest Bag On Earth

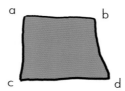

1. Bring corners a and c together in a square knot.

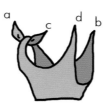

2. Bring corners b and d together in a square knot.

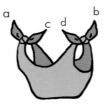

3. Test your knots for strength.

Plastic Bags Are Killing Us

Plastic shopping bags embody perhaps everything bad about our wasteful culture. How many brand new plastic bags do we use in a day and throw out that same day? I was shocked when someone asked me to think about the fact that every plastic bag I have ever used in my life will either remain in a landfill somewhere or be blowing around in nature for the next 1000 years. Even then, I found it very hard to remember to bring along my canvas grocery bag to the store every time.

The solution is to always keep a few wrapping scarves in my purse and car for any kind of shopping I end up doing, whether it is for groceries, office supplies, or clothes. You can make a bag and put your items in the bag, or you can lay the scarf out flat and have the checked out groceries or other merchandise put in the middle. Then you will only need to bring the opposite corners together to tie up your bundle in The Lotus Wrap (page 31).

My favorite shopping bag uses a nylon wrapping scarf to make a hobo-style bag. It is lightweight and strong, yet stylish at the same time. Either way, don't forget that you can adjust the knots when you get to the car so that nothing spills out during the car ride home.

The Hobo Bag

Here is another occasion when I found myself mesmerized by the simple transformation of a wrapping scarf into a bona-fide bag. The process of folding, tying, flipping, and shaking was nothing short of magical. What a difference a little know-how makes!

To make a grocery bag like the one shown on the opposite page, use a large wrap that is about 45" x 45".

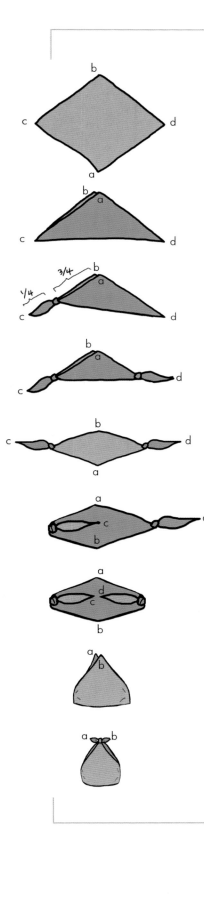

1. Lay the wrapping scarf flat on the diagonal.

2. Bring corner a up to corner b to make a triangle.

3. Measure approximately ¼ of the way up on the side c, b and tie a single knot.

4. Do the same thing on the side d, a. Make sure that the two ends c and d are fairly equal in length and tighten the knots.

5. Separate corners a and b and open the triangle so that corner a is at the bottom.

6. Flip the whole wrapping scarf so that corner a is now at the top. Fold corner c toward the center of the wrapping scarf.

7. Fold corner d toward the center of the wrapping scarf.

8. Bring corners a and b together. Hold the wrapping scarf by corners a and b and shake to form your pouch.

9. Tie corners a and b together in a secure square knot.

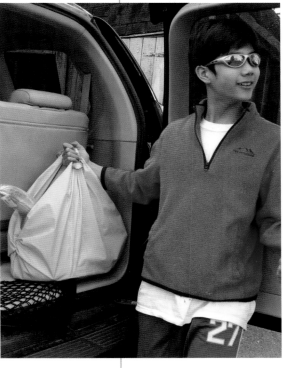

The Side Knot Purse

This is an elegant variation of the Hobo Bag. Follow all the steps for the Hobo Bag except the final step of tying the handles together. Then follow the instructions below to make a delightful little purse perfect for day or evening.

1. Take corner b and tie a single knot halfway down the bag. The placement of your knot will determine how large the pouch of your bag will be.

2. Repeat for corner a, making sure that the two lengths of fabric are about equal.

3. Tie corners a and b together in a square knot.

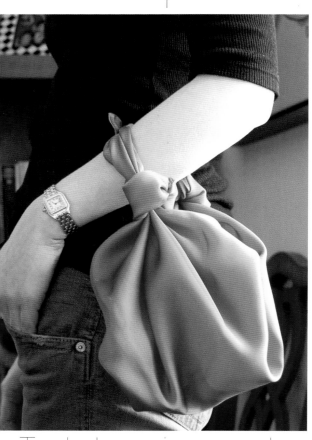

To make this size purse, use a medium wrap that is about 35" x 35".

The Half-Knot Purse

This is another variation of the Hobo Bag. In the final step, tie a half knot instead of a square knot. Pull the half knot until it is half way down the bag. Bring the ends together and tie a square knot at the top to form your handle. Loosen the half knot to access the pouch.

You can control the color of your bows by carefully monitoring the second half of your square knot (see page 27).

The Day Bag with Bamboo Handles

Don't you love bamboo? Not only is it the fastest growing woody plant on the planet, it's also one of the strongest building materials around. Asians have been using bamboo for building, decoration, medicine, food, and more for over 5000 years. In fact, the Damyang Bamboo Museum in Korea is the only museum of its kind and exhibits many examples of antique and modern bamboo ware.

Strong, fast growing, and beautiful to boot, bamboo is the answer to a lot of our environmental concerns. For this project, make sure you get the real bamboo handles and not the plastic replicas.

To make the Day Bag shown above, use a large wrap that is about 42" x 42". The bamboo rings are eight inches in diameter.

To make the bag shown at right, use a medium sized wrap that is about 28" x 28". The bamboo rings are five inches in diameter.

Anchor the wrapping scarf onto the first ring without being too concerned about how the knot looks.

After tying wrap onto the second ring, come back to the first side and retie with a nice square knot.

When both sides are secured, put your hand in the bag and gently punch the pouch to test knots and give the bag shape.

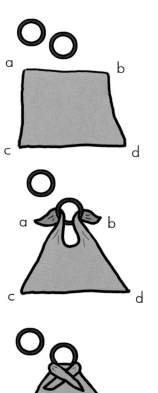

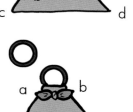

1. Bring corners a and b through the bamboo handle.

2. Bring corners a and b around to meet in front of the wrapping scarf.

3. Tie corners a and b in a square knot.

4. Take the other bamboo handle and repeat with corners c and d.

To make an adorable little wristlet, try using a small wrapping scarf about 22" x 22" with small 4" rings.

Photo by Miriam Ri

My friend Esther had this lovely birthday cake custom made by Perfect Endings Bakery in Armonk. We were all perfectly charmed!

The Handbag Wrap

A great way to give new life to an old handbag is to give it a fabulous wrapping scarf makeover. The ideal handbag for this project would be slightly narrower at the top than at the bottom, with two stiff handles. Crafty chic!

1. Place handbag in the center of the wrap.

2. Raise corners a and b and loop through the handle as shown.

3. Roll/fold corners a and b down so that contrasting color is showing.

4. Bring corners a and b around to meet in front of the bag and tie loosely in a square knot. This will serve as an anchor while tying the other side.

5. Take corners c and d and repeat steps 2-5, this time taking care to fold and tie square knot neatly.

6. Go back to the other side and retie neatly.

The handbag shown above measures 12" x 9" x 4" and was wrapped with a 45" x 45" wrapping scarf.

The Backpack

This clever makeshift backpack consists of two wrapping scarves, one for the bag and one for the strap. Make this in a jiffy when you find you have things to carry but need both hands free. I once found myself in the city struggling with heavy bags digging into my hands when I decided to make a backpack with my wrapping scarves. I dumped everything in and felt a wonderful connection with my ancestors who probably did the same thing in a bit of a different setting!

To make a back pack as shown, use two large wraps that are about 45" x 45".

A smaller wrap used for the straps will result in shorter straps.

The Backpack

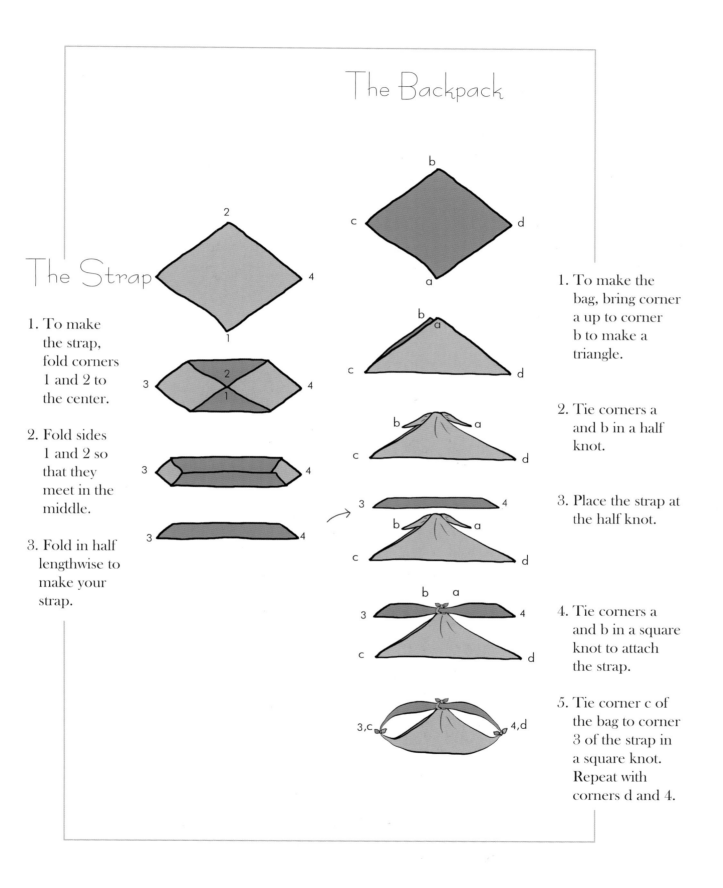

The Strap

1. To make the strap, fold corners 1 and 2 to the center.

2. Fold sides 1 and 2 so that they meet in the middle.

3. Fold in half lengthwise to make your strap.

1. To make the bag, bring corner a up to corner b to make a triangle.

2. Tie corners a and b in a half knot.

3. Place the strap at the half knot.

4. Tie corners a and b in a square knot to attach the strap.

5. Tie corner c of the bag to corner 3 of the strap in a square knot. Repeat with corners d and 4.

Décor & Other Uses

The Tissue Box Frock

The Picnic Wrap

The Pleated Planter

The Bowl Wrap & Carry

The Pillow Cover

The Basket Liner Wrap

The Artwork Wrap & Carry

Decorative Wrapping for Your Home

Y ou can use a beautiful wrapping scarf in so many ways around your home. Your cardboard tissue box will get a beautiful new frock and your old throw pillow can be stylishly updated in seconds. I love to wrap up food that I've prepared for a potluck lunch in a wrapping scarf. Because of the custom fit, I can stack several containers and know that nothing is going to move or shift around while being transported. Whatever needs a little covering or decorative touch will get an instant makeover with a wrapping scarf, though you may find yourself stealing from a planter or tissue box when you need to wrap a gift at the last minute!

Like favorite clothing that gets old and ratty, an old wrapping scarf still has many good uses. Sometimes I'm a little reluctant to use a brand-new pristine wrapping scarf to transport my stack of food for a picnic or to line an old basket. That's when I'll look for my older more worn scarves to do the job. Reusing is always more eco-friendly than recycling.

The Tissue Box Frock

Ugly cardboard tissue boxes used to be a pet peeve and I tried to hide them as much as possible. Now all my tissue boxes are proudly decked out in elegant wrapping scarves and displayed conveniently throughout the house.

 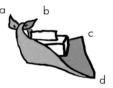

1. Place tissue box in the center of the wrapping scarf.

2. Tie corners a and b in a square knot.

3. Tie corners b and d in a square knot. Tuck away any loose fabric.

This very functional wrapping technique can also be used on planters (see page 2). Upside down, it can serve as a dust cover for just about anything from a toaster to a sewing machine.

For this standard size tissue box, we used a 22" square wrapping scarf.

The Picnic Wrap

Taking food to a picnic or bringing dinner to a sick friend would always involve a mad dash around the house, looking for the right disposable bag to fit the kind of containers I was using. If the bag was too small, it would rip, if it was too big, the food would tip over during the trip and make a big mess.

A wrapping scarf tied with the Lotus Wrap will give one container or stack of containers a perfect fit every time. At a picnic, a large wrap can serve double duty and be used to sit on.

The wrapping scarf is also useful as a lunch bag. The scarf can be untied and used as a placemat until everything needs to be wrapped up again to take home. The knots at the top serve as a very useful handle.

To wrap a few containers (above and opposite), use a large wrap that is about 44" x 44".

To wrap a lunch (right), use a medium wrap that is about 27" x 27".

The Pleated Planter

Make your own variations! At my nephew Otis' birthday party, we skipped the pleating for a simplified version of this wrap.

To wrap 6" to 8" planters as shown, use a medium scarf that is about 27" x 27".

Orchids are the ultimate houseplant for me. My friend got me hooked when she assured me that orchids are secretly the lazyman's flower of choice. Unlike other houseplants, orchids require very infrequent waterings and will actually perish under too rigorous a watering schedule. I give my orchids a nice soaking in the kitchen sink every two to three weeks and enjoy their long lasting blooms and reblooms.

The pleating in this beautiful method of dressing up a planter may take a few tries to master, but don't worry if you can't get it just right. It looks just as good when you fan out the pleats for a looser, more voluminous look.

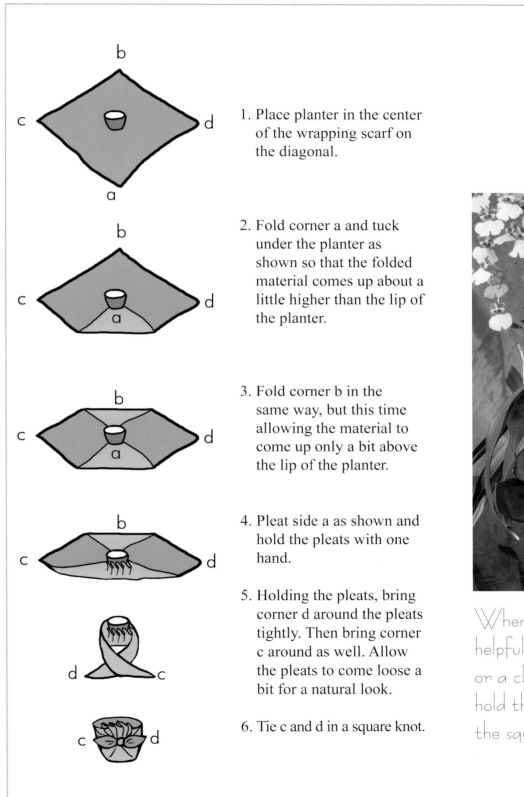

1. Place planter in the center of the wrapping scarf on the diagonal.

2. Fold corner a and tuck under the planter as shown so that the folded material comes up about a little higher than the lip of the planter.

3. Fold corner b in the same way, but this time allowing the material to come up only a bit above the lip of the planter.

4. Pleat side a as shown and hold the pleats with one hand.

5. Holding the pleats, bring corner d around the pleats tightly. Then bring corner c around as well. Allow the pleats to come loose a bit for a natural look.

6. Tie c and d in a square knot.

When pleating, it might be helpful to use a clothespin or a clip of some kind to hold the pleats while you tie the square knot.

The Bowl Wrap & Carry

Here's a great way to add a handle to an ordinary bowl or dress up a boring bowl for gift-giving.

If you would like the contents of your bowl to be covered, just lift up the flaps of the wrap inside the bowl and place items under the flaps.

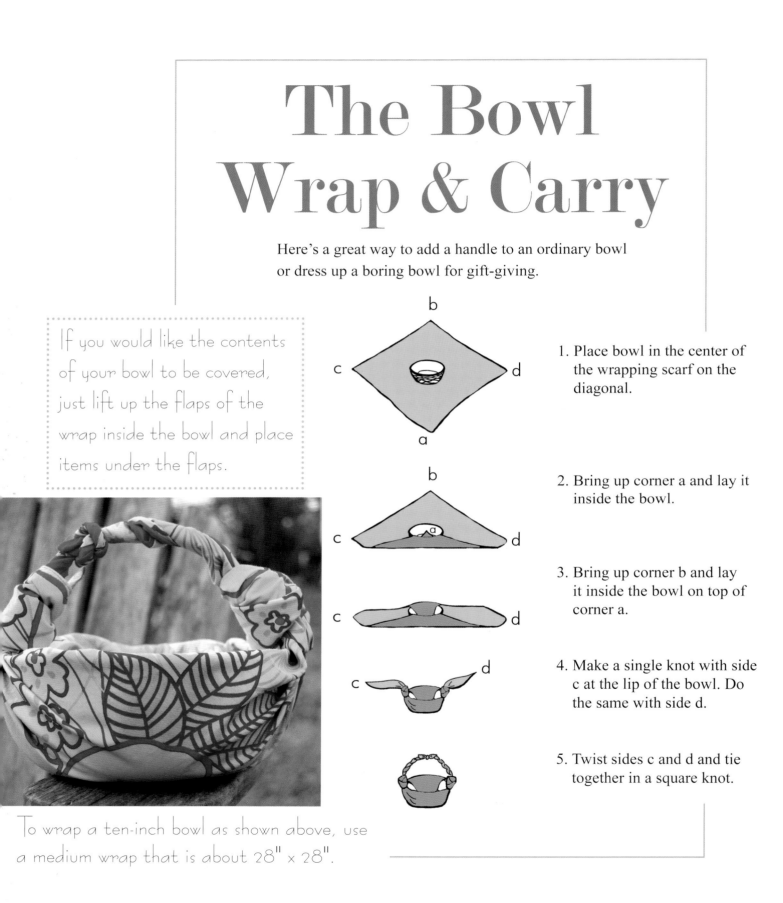

1. Place bowl in the center of the wrapping scarf on the diagonal.

2. Bring up corner a and lay it inside the bowl.

3. Bring up corner b and lay it inside the bowl on top of corner a.

4. Make a single knot with side c at the lip of the bowl. Do the same with side d.

5. Twist sides c and d and tie together in a square knot.

To wrap a ten-inch bowl as shown above, use a medium wrap that is about 28" x 28".

The Pillow Cover

With the changing of seasons or just for fun, bring a new splash of color to your home décor by wrapping some throw pillows. This is the same technique as the Bow Tie Wrap with a slight variation at step 4.

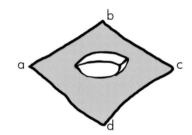

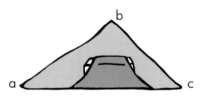

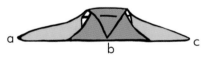

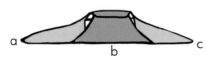

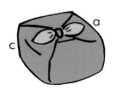

1. Place pillow in the center of the wrapping scarf on the diagonal.

2. Raise corner d and drape over the pillow.

3. Repeat with corner b.

4. Fold corner b under at the center of the pillow.

5. Tie corners a and c in a square knot.

To wrap a 19" x 12" pillow as shown, use a large 42" x 42" wrapping scarf.

The Basket Liner Wrap

This is a quick and handy way to line a basket. You get a custom fit every time! A cotton wrap is great for everyday practical usage. For parties, try using a more festive wrap to line a basket full of beautiful favors.

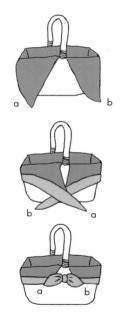

1. Place wrapping scarf square in the center of the basket completely lining the inside. Let the edges hang over the outside of the basket.

2. Fold up the edges of the wrapping scarf once or twice so that the reverse side is showing.

3. Tie corners a and b in a square knot. Repeat on the other side.

It's okay to have the two bows be different sizes. If you'd like them to be symmetricial, try anchoring on the first side loosely then coming back to fix it after the other side is finished.

To wrap a basket as shown above, use a large wrap that is about 45" x 45".

The Artwork Wrap & Carry

As an artist, I use this method whenever I need to transport my paintings, whether I'm headed to the frame shop or delivering to a patron. If your picture is delicate or if you are transporting a frame with glass, wrap with bubble wrap first or use several wrapping scarves, flipping upside down for each subsequent layer.

Untying this wrap for the big "reveal" is always a treat!

To wrap an 18 x 24 inch frame as shown on the opposite page, use a large wrap that is about 45" x 45".

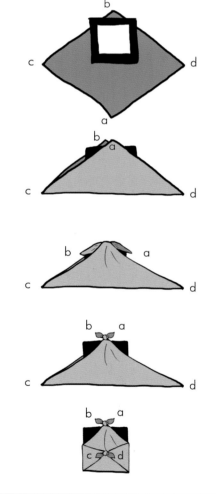

1. Lay artwork on the diagonal at the top center of the wrapping scarf. Leave a little space at the top

2. Bring up corner a to cover the artwork. Make sure the fabric is flush with the bottom edge of the artwork.

3. Tie corners a and b in a square knot. Use this square knot as your handle for carrying.

4. Bring corners c and d together and tie in a square knot.

A Quick Guide to Making Your Own Wrapping Scarf

From super frugal to eco-luxe, a wrapping scarf lifestyle can take many shapes and forms. Here are some suggestions for quick and easy ways you can start wrapping up your world today.

Use What You've Got!

Here are a few items you may have around the house that could be used as a wrapping scarf right now:

- An old fabric napkin that's not too bulky makes a nice wrap for a kitchen-related gift.
- A bandana is great for wrapping up a small container and utensils for a packed lunch.
- A square tablecloth is perfect for wrapping up a stack of food and drinks when going on a picnic.
- An old silk scarf that is square in shape works great for wrapping a gift.

Make a Single Layered Wrap

1. Choose a piece of fabric that is strong but not too heavy.
2. Cut the fabric into a perfect square.
3. Hem the edges all the way around.

Make a Double Layered Wrap

1. Choose two coordinating pieces of fabric.
2. Put the two pieces together and tie a corner in a single knot to make sure it is not too thick for wrapping.
3. Cut the two pieces into same-size squares.
4. Layer the fabric with the wrong sides facing out.
5. Pin the two pieces of fabric together all the way around.
6. Stitch all the way around leaving a 2" hole at the end. Trim corners diagonally to reduce bulk.
7. Take a corner of the wrap and guide it all the way through the hole until the whole wrap is flipped inside out.
8. Stitch the hole shut and press the seams.

Size Guide

14" - 16" Square
Wrap a holiday ornament
Wrap potpourri to create a sachet
Wrap a ring or bracelet box

20" - 22" Square
Wrap a few CDs
Wrap paper back books
Make a Tissue Box Frock

27" - 29" Square
Wrap a shirt box
Wrap a wine bottle or two
Make a small purse or knitting bag

36" - 38" Square
Wrap wine bottles
Make bags
Wrap a dress box

42" - 45" Square
Wrap wine bottles
Make a large Hobo Bag
Wrap a rolled-up poster